Teach your Child To Read: A step-by-step Parenting guide On How To Teach A Child To Read

By

Benjamin Moore

Table Of Content

Introduction

Teaching a child to read is a rewarding and developmental experience for both the parent and the child. You can begin teaching your child to read at home, whether you homeschool your children or simply want to give your child a head start. Your child will be reading in no time if you provide them with the right tools and strategies.

Chapter One

Begin Early

You Should Read to Your Child On a Regular basis

It is difficult to learn anything without exposure to it, as it is with everything else. You should read to your child on a regular basis to get them interested in reading. If possible, begin when they are infants and continue through their school years. Read books with stories they can understand; at a young age, this may lead to 3-4 small books per day.

Books that combine other senses besides hearing aid your young child's comprehension of the story as you read it. Read a lot of books that have pictures, tactile pages, sounds, or accompanying scents, for example.

Try reading them books that may be a little difficult for them to understand but have an interesting or engaging story.

Pose Interactive Questions

Reading comprehension can be learned even before your child learns to read. Ask them questions about the characters or the plot as you read stories to them aloud. For a toddler, these could be questions such as "Do you notice the dog? What is the name of the dog? ". As the reading level rises, so will the difficulty of the questions. Asking open-ended questions about stories can help your child learn critical thinking skills. You may not hear complex verbal responses from your child until he or she is four or five years old, but keep asking and be patient.

Make Books Readily Available

It's useless if you have books around but they're in places where your child can't easily get to them. Keep books near the ground and in common play areas so that your child associates them with play activities.

Because your child will be touching and reading the books frequently, choose ones with wipeable pages that aren't overly sentimental. Pop-up books might not be the best choice for small children.

A fancy bookshelf may appear to be the most appealing option, but until your child starts school, focus on the functional aspects of book storage.

Create a reading nook next to the bookshelf. Set out some beanbags, pillows, and comfortable chairs for reading. The top of the bookshelf can be used to store cups and snacks for reading.

Lead By Example

By reading for yourself, you can demonstrate to your child that reading is enjoyable and worthwhile. Spend at least ten minutes a day reading when your child is present, so they see you doing it on your own. Even if you're not a voracious reader, find something to read - a magazine, a newspaper, or a cookbook are all acceptable options. They'll soon be interested in reading on their own as a result of seeing you do it.

Participate in your reading time with your child. If you're reading something appropriate for children, tell them about it. To help them connect the lines on the page with the sounds that form words, point to words on the page.

Obtain Library Access

This can be accomplished in two ways: build your own mini-library at home by collecting dozens of books at your child's reading level, or go to the local public library together on a weekly basis to check out books. Having a variety of books on hand (especially if your child is older) will increase their interest in reading and help them incorporate more vocabulary into their knowledge base.

However, don't refuse a request to re-read a favorite book simply because it's been read a dozen times.

Begin Making word-sound Associations

Before you get into the alphabet and sound specifics, make sure your child understands that the lines on the page correspond to the words you're saying. While reading aloud to them, point to each word on the page as you say it. This will assist your child in understanding the pattern of words/lines on the page that correspond to the words you speak in terms of length and sound.

Avoid The Use Of Flashcards

Some businesses have advertised specialized flashcards to assist babies, toddlers, and preschool-aged children in learning to read. Flashcards are not the most useful or effective technique for teaching reading skills in general. Reading stories to your child will be far more beneficial than flashcards. "Reading aloud to young children, especially in an engaging manner, promotes emergent literacy and language development and strengthens the parent-child relationship. Furthermore, it can foster a love of reading, which is more important than improving specific literacy skills."

Chapter 2

Teach The Fundamentals

Teach Your Child The ABCs

When your child has mastered word recognition, start breaking down words into individual letters. Although the alphabet song is the most traditional method of teaching the alphabet, experiment with other methods. Explain each letter by name, but don't worry about incorporating the sounds the letters make just yet.

Lowercase letters should be taught first. Capital letters account for only 5% of all letters used in English writing. As a result, focus more on teaching lowercase letters. Lowercase letters play a far greater role in the development of reading skills.

Make each letter out of play-doh, play a toss game (in which the child throws a beanbag/ball onto a specific letter on the floor), or fish for foam letters in the bathtub. These are all interactive games that promote growth on multiple levels.

Improve Your Phonemic Awareness

Associating a spoken sound with a letter or letter-pair is a critical step in teaching reading. This is referred to as phonemic awareness. The 26 letters in our alphabet produce 44 speech sounds, and each sound must be taught in tandem with its letter(s). This includes the long and short sounds made by each letter, as well as the specialized sounds made by some combined letters (such as 'ch' and'sh').

Concentrate on one letter/part/sound at a time. Working at a steady pace through all of the speech sounds will help you avoid confusion and lay a solid foundation.

Give real-world examples of each speech sound, such as how the letter 'A' makes the 'ah' sound at the beginning of the word 'apple.' This can be turned into a guessing game by saying an easy word (like apple) and having the child guess which letter it begins with.

Use games that combine critical thinking on the part of the child to determine sound/letter correlations, similar to those used when teaching the alphabet. See the list above for inspiration, but replace the words with sounds.

When words are broken down into their smallest parts, it is easier for children to develop phonemic awareness. This can be accomplished through the clapping game (clapping out each syllable in a word) or by breaking words down into their individual letters.

Teach Your Child to Recite Rhymes

Rhyming, in addition to teaching basic English words, teaches phonemic awareness and letter recognition. Read nursery rhymes to your child, and then make lists of simple rhymes like mop, top, flop, pop, and cop. Your child will begin to recognize the patterns of sounds produced when certain letters are combined - in this case, the 'o-p' sound.

Using Explicit Phonics, Teach your Child to Read

Children are traditionally taught to recognize words based on their size, the first and last letters, and the overall sound. Working from the largest piece down, this method of teaching is known as implicit phonics. However, studies have shown that teaching each word in its smallest parts and building them up into a full word - explicit phonics - dramatically increases readable vocabulary (from 900 words to 3000 words by third grade). Help your child learn to read by having them sound out each individual letter without first looking at the entire word.

Don't introduce explicit phonics until your child has mastered phonemic awareness. If they can't quickly associate sounds with letters or letter pairs, they'll need more practice before moving on to full words.

Allow Your Child To Practice Decoding

Decoding, also known as sounding out words, is when a child reads a word by making the sounds of each individual letter rather than attempting to read the entire word at once. Reading is divided into two stages: decoding/reading a word and comprehending its meaning. Expect your child to focus on decoding and sounding out word parts rather than recognizing and comprehending words just yet.

Instead of using whole stories or books, have your child read from word lists or a basic story (not focusing on the plot). This is another excellent opportunity to practice rhymes.

Decoding aloud usually helps the child (and you) learn how to say the word. If necessary, have them break it up with clapping.

Do not be too strict about how the child pronounces the sounds. Regional accents and poor auditory skills make it difficult for children to say most sounds correctly. Accept a reasonable attempt. Recognize that learning sounds is only a prerequisite for learning to read; it is not the end goal.

Don't Be Concerned About Grammar

Preschoolers, kindergartners, and first graders think in very concrete terms and cannot handle complex concepts. Most English-speaking children have an excellent grasp of grammar by the age of four, and they will eventually learn all of the formal grammatical rules. At this point, you should focus solely on the mechanical skill of reading, that is, learning to decode new words and memorize them in order to develop fluency.

Create a Sight Word Archive

Certain words in the English vocabulary are frequently used but do not follow standard phonics rules. These words are known as sight words' because they are easier to remember by shape association rather than sound. 'They,"she,' 'an,"said,' and 'the' are examples of sight words. The entire list of sight words, known as the Dolch list, can be found online and divided into sections to work through.

Display sight words on a piece of paper to your child. Allow them to copy it, and then ask them to tell you what the word is after you've told them.

Chapter 3

Increase Difficulty

Start Telling Your Child Complete Stories

Your child will almost certainly be in school by the time they can read and will be given their own reading material by their teachers. Encourage them to read the entire story by using explicit phonics and recognizing vocabulary. As their word recognition improves, they will be able to comprehend story plots and meanings more fully.

Allow your child to look at the pictures; doing so does not constitute cheating. Image and word association is an important aspect of vocabulary development.

Allow Your Child To Tell You The Story

After each reading session, ask your child to tell you about the story. Try to get them to be specific, but don't expect a lengthy response. Using puppets to represent characters in the story so your child can describe it to you through them is an easy and fun way to help encourage this.

Inquire About The Stories

Ask your child questions about what they've just read, just like you did when you were reading stories to them. It will be difficult for them at first to think critically about word meanings and the development of character development and plot (or the semblance of those things in the most basic of stories), but they will eventually develop the necessary skills to answer questions.

Make a list of questions that your child can read; their ability to read and understand the provided questions is nearly as important as their ability to answer the questions themselves.

Begin with direct questions, such as 'who was the main character in the book?' rather than more abstract questions, such as 'why was the main character upset?'

Incorporate Writing Into Your Reading

Reading is a prerequisite for writing, but as your child develops reading skills, have them practice writing as well. Children learn to read more quickly and easily if they also learn to write. The motor memory of the letters, as well as hearing and seeing them written, will reinforce new learning. As a result, teach your child how to write letters and words.

Your child's reading ability will improve as he or she learns to spell by decoding and sounding out words. But go slowly and don't expect perfection.

Continue To Read To Your Child

You should continue to promote reading to/with your child on a daily basis, just as you taught them the joy of reading before they knew how. When they can see words as you read them, rather than struggling to do both at the same time, they will develop a stronger phonemic awareness.

Have Your Child Read Aloud To You

When your child reads aloud, you'll get a better sense of their reading ability, and they'll be forced to slow down to correctly sound out words. Stopping your child to correct them while they're reading, on the other hand, can disrupt their train of thought and make understanding what they're reading more difficult.

Reading aloud isn't just for stories; whenever you're around words, have your child sound them out to you. Road signs are an excellent example of something your child will see on a daily basis and can practice reading to you.

Conclusion

Learning to read can be a lengthy process, so it is never too early to start preparing a child. While learning to read is an important milestone, it is critical that the process be enjoyable and engaging for the child. Reading should be something that the child enjoys and can use to expand their knowledge through books. If you are patient and make the learning process a fun way to spend time together, your child will have the best chance of learning to read and love books.

About The Author

Benjamin Moore (born January 5, 1984) is a Canadian-American motivational public speaker and self-development author. He is the author of over eighty books that have been translated into dozens of languages.